YOUR MAINE LANDS

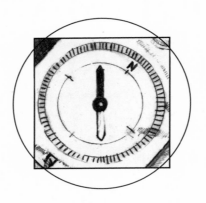

YOUR MAINE LANDS

REFLECTIONS OF A MAINE GUIDE

TOM HANRAHAN

Illustrated by Kelly Thorndike

With a Foreword by
John Elias Baldacci

Polar Bear & Company
Solon, Maine

Polar Bear & Company
P.O. Box 311, Solon, Maine 04979 U.S.A.
207-643-2795 www.polarbearandco.com

12 11 10 09 08   3 4 5 6 7 8 9
All artwork by Kelly Thorndike; photo page 26 by Ramona du Houx;
all other photos by author.
Cover design by Ramona du Houx; cover photo by Dan Cashman.

All outdoor recreational activities include inherent risks and conditions are
constantly changing. Nothing in this book is intended to promote a particular
activity, at any particular time, for any particular individual. Readers of this
book must assess their own abilities, and make independent determinations
about existing conditions and participation in outdoor recreational activities.
Use of the information in this book is at the sole risk of the reader.

Library of Congress Cataloging-in-Publication Data

Hanrahan, Tom.
Your Maine lands : reflections of a Maine guide / Tom Hanrahan ; illustrated
by Kelly Thorndike ; with a foreword by John Elias Baldacci. -- 1st ed.
p. cm.
Summary: "On behalf of Maine's Department of Conservation, a master
Maine guide introduces the free amenities of the nearly one million acres of
Maine's public lands, including hunting and fishing, with advice on how to
prepare for a visit to the North Maine Woods"--Provided by publisher.
ISBN 978-1-882190-91-1 (pbk. : alk. paper)
1. Outdoor recreation--Maine--Guidebooks. 2. Maine--Guidebooks. I. Title.
GV191.42.M2H37 2008
917.41'0444--dc22
2008034376

Manufactured in the U.S.A. by Thomson-Shore, Inc., an employee-owned
company—certified by the Forest Stewardship Council and a member of the
Green Press Initiative—using soy ink and acid free, recycled paper of archival
quality, at paper permanence specifications defined by ANSI.NISO standard
Z39.48-992: "The ability of paper to last several hundred years without significant
deterioration under normal use and storage conditions in libraries and archives."

For El-Snake-a-Toro

Contents

Foreword

During my tenure as governor, the state has added some 1.5 million acres to the public trust, from some of the world's premier bird watching areas to panoramic ocean vistas. Some areas are pristine wilderness, and many are readily accessible to the public.

This is an accomplishment we can all be proud of. Mainers treasure the wildness of our state. These public lands represent a lasting commitment to protecting our natural treasures.

Mainers also treasure tradition. Our outdoor legacy is broad and deep. Hunting and fishing, canoeing and camping, hiking and bird watching, trapping, and cross-country skiing—all of these recreational activities are permitted and encouraged in these public places.

These are YOUR lands, for you and your children and your children's children. Parts of Maine that will remain protected forever.

Visitors can depend on returning to the same places year after year and know they will remain the same, beautiful and unspoiled.

I hope you enjoy these spots, and remember, they belong to all the people of Maine.

John Elias Baldacci
Governor

Special Places

Public lands. It sounds very governmental, yet what it means to millions of people in America and in Maine is, special places. I have spent a lifetime tramping the trails of our public lands in pursuit of outdoor experiences. During those hours and days, I have found solace, comfort, and sometimes a large fish or a partridge or a view from a mountaintop that was ingested within my soul. Many of these adventures have been with family and friends, and some of those folks are no longer on this earth or have moved far away. This connection with the lands and the rivers forged a bond that will never be broken.

I have had a wonderful privilege to be the commissioner of the Maine Department of Conservation for over six years. It has been the best job that I have had in my life. During that time we have added over one million acres of land to the public trust in both fee and easement. This chore has been a great deal of work by hundreds of people across this great state. The end result is that many more memories and many more adventures are waiting to be had on your public lands here in Maine. Programs like Land for Maine's Future have assisted us in putting hundreds of thousands of acres in permanent conservation for our children's children.

The department has requested Tom Hanrahan, a noted Maine outdoor writer and master guide, to put together his stories of his adventures on public lands. This book is a delight to read, and hopefully you may use it to put together your next adventure with family and friends on your public lands in the great State of Maine.

To learn more about Maine's public lands, visit the department's Web site at www.parksandlands.com.

Patrick K. McGowan
Commissioner
Dept. of Conservation

1. GOING PUBLIC

W HEN Patrick McGowan first approached me to write something about Maine's public lands, I was surprised to discover how little I knew of the nearly one million acres. In an era when every day something new is reported regarding development of the great North Maine Woods, it was fascinating to learn there was this much protected land.

I remember my first thought about public land. I was staying at a remote camp owned by Matt Libby and passed a public preserve named Telos. "I should check that out because that might be my future hunting ground," I said to myself.

In the summer of 2007, I started traveling about the state visiting public lands, and I was genuinely surprised how little I knew about the diverse nature of these properties.

First of all, Maine is BIG. I've driven thousands of miles discovering this "secret" part of Maine, and one could make an avocation of visiting all these places. On your gazetteer there are checked blue lines to indicate a public preserve and once you start paying attention, they spring out from the page.

EVERY ONE FOR YOUR USE, FREE OF CHARGE.

I made it a point to ask my friends and fellow guides if they had visited or hunted or fished these lands, and few knew the extent of these public places. And when I did find people who knew about these special sites, they begged me not to write about them!

That should tell you something.

From Deboullie to Nahmakanta to Cutler Coast, Scraggly Lake to Duck Lake and the Unknowns, Maine provides a diverse offering of public lands. Just about any recreational activity you can think of is available and few activities are not allowed. You can hunt and fish and tent and hike and canoe and go bird watching. You can take your ATV or snowmobile and ride.

So enjoy!

2. ON BEING ALONE

I spend more time alone than anybody I know. If you have not spent any time alone lately, try starting with one day of solitude. It will give you a taste for what is to come, and by that I mean some extended time all by yourself. As Van Morrison would say, "into the mystic."

One of the great things about the big Maine woods is you can be alone without too much effort. You can get a camp and be isolated quite readily, or you can hike and camp and be alone and on the move, both.

It's not easy. We are so conditioned to be constantly interacting with one another and the TV and the computer and the pager and fax and palm pilot and more—that solitude comes as a shock to the system. I liken it to a clock that is so over-wound it doesn't tick. Once it is freed, well, ticking commences again. You don't know what you are missing when you are so over-wound, and once you free that spinning wheel, all sorts of ticking takes place that can fascinate and confound.

When you start, you will be a little nutty from it. There is no one to talk to. There is nothing to watch or listen to, other than the sound of the wind through the trees and maybe a thunderstorm. Perhaps you will stop and twiddle your thumbs. Fine. It's a start. Your first revelation will likely be that this is something absolutely unique and vital. You are in the company of one person and one person only, and that is you. Maybe you don't know you. Well, pursue solitude and you will get to know you!

I stumbled on solitude.

My wife joins me for bird season, but then she goes home. I wanted to stay up at camp for deer season, so I did. Bang! She gets in the car and leaves. I am left in a camp that is instantly solitary and empty. I want to chase after and say, "Come back, come back! I am LONELY!"

Already.

Those first twenty-four hours, those are the toughest ones. If

you can get past those, with the feelings of shock and dread, you'll have gotten past what I call "Phase I" and into "Phase II." Phase II is where you begin to have a little fun and mostly recover from the initial shock of making the plunge. You will cook by yourself and sleep by yourself and talk to yourself, if you wish. Nobody will answer unless you talk back to yourself. It's comical, really.

But being alone can be really scary, and a psychiatrist I know says, how well you cope with being alone, all alone, utterly alone, is a pretty good measure of your mental health. If you can't hack being alone, that's OK, but you might want to ask yourself what it is that is so threatening about being alone that you cannot tolerate it.

Being in the woods all alone has its own particular terror. It's dark and foreboding. I would come home to camp at dusk and surely want to be in camp with the lights on by the time the sun petered out. It gets so dark out in the woods you can put your hand in front of your face and not see it. Now, that is dark.

But as time went by, I would go for a walk at night, and it reminded me of scuba diving at night, so dark and inky black.

As time goes by—and you will experience this, believe me—the whole trip becomes magical. And you reach a peaceful place. This place will change you forever. And all you need to do to get there is commit to being alone. The longest I have gone is two weeks. But I don't fear it anymore; I welcome it. Like I said, if you can make it past those first twenty-four hours, you have a real shot at going further and "into the mystic."

Good luck!

3. OCEAN VIEW SNOWMOBILING

I am gliding along on my snowmobile in a frozen forest of ash, oak, and maple. In the distance I can see something few riders ever get to see from their skidoos. The boundless Atlantic Ocean. Stretching out as far as the eye can see.

I am blissfully, magnificently alone. There is a foot of fresh snow, and the temperature is in the mid 30s. Bright sunshine makes it feel even warmer. It doesn't get much better than this in mid-February in Maine.

I encounter no one all day long.

Stopping to admire the sea, I am overwhelmed. The water is the color of slate and is dotted by small islands colored a dark green.

Surrounded by some six thousand acres of parkland, my snow machine powers through deer and moose habitat, home to fisher and bobcat, hawk and osprey, fox and snowshoe hare.

I am deep inside Camden Hills State Park in Camden, Maine, a town most notable for wealthy retirees, million-dollar coastal homes, and being a nest of former CIA operatives. The park is only three miles north of town. In summer it is visited by more than two hundred thousand people. It encompasses parts of two counties and is part of the million acres of public land in Maine. Land which is nearly entirely earmarked for traditional uses—hunting and fishing, hiking and canoeing, trapping and snowmobiling, ATV and snowshoe enthusiasts, cross-country skiers and bird watchers.

Cost of my daylong sojourn?

Not a dime.

For entrance to the state parks in summer, admission is $3.00. In winter it is free. The rest of the public Maine lands cost nothing to use. "One of the best deals anywhere," says state conservation Commissioner Patrick McGowan. "We want people to know there is a significant amount of state land that everyone can have access to, beautiful places—many of them wilderness areas—where they can recreate and enjoy the great outdoors for free."

Camden Hills offers some twenty trails for visitors to use and forms a mountain biker's and hiker's paradise. Ranging in difficulty from easy to strenuous, there are trips lasting in duration from ten minutes to three hours. One particularly beautiful trail, of moderate difficulty, offers sweeping views of the ocean, the surrounding hills and lakes.

There are views of eight-hundred-foot cliffs, climbing high above Megunticook Lake, and excellent views of Penobscot Bay. There are bike trails that run through oak-and-spruce forests over three mountains, old carriage roads, and a meandering path that winds its way through blueberry fields and mature forests. The highest peak, reaching 1,380 feet, covers Megunticook Mountain's ridge and wooded summit.

My day started in midmorning and lasted well into the late afternoon. I would ride some and then stop, reveling in the peace and quiet. A snowshoe hare had left its tracks on the path, and I passed a lodge built in the 1930s by the Civilian Conservation Corps. The park traces its roots to Depression-era federal programs and early efforts to develop state park systems nationwide.

"We get a lot of people who come here to exercise in a pristine, natural environment," says Bill Elliot, the park superintendent. "We've had a lot of snow this year, so we also get quite a few snowmobilers."

But I encounter none. With my snowshoes tied to the sled, I stop to strap them on, the better to traverse the trails that have not been broken by snowmobile tracks. It's hard to believe I am only a few miles outside downtown Camden, but I am.

"We have 107 campsites available in summer, and during the

lobster and blues festivals we are really mobbed," says Elliot.
"Those two festivals have really gotten the park into the mix, and
to be honest, it's a lot of fun."

It's also a safe park, as all the trails are well marked and carefully
maintained. The snowmobile cruised effortlessly along, and
everywhere I looked I could see the ocean through the forest.

"It is a special place," noted park ranger Pete Carpenter. "In
summer the turkey vultures ride the thermals, and a lot of folks
come to watch them float through the sky."

Perhaps because it is a state park, not many hunters are aware
that outstanding deer hunting is to be had during November.
Portions of the same trails used for hiking can also be used to
hunt whitetails. "We don't get many deer hunters, and I think that's
because not many hunters are aware hunting is permitted here,"
says Elliot. "But the hunting is good, and it's a safe place to hunt,
without homes or other dwellings close nearby."

I ended up my day with a staggering view of the ocean from a
high rise. The only sound was the crunching of snow made by the
weight of my snowshoes. I had a great time, all alone in the woods,
and it didn't cost me a dime.

Nor did I encounter one NO TRESPASSING sign.

4. ON HUNTING

Maine's boreal forest provides hunters with a diverse bounty of
game. I love the fact that I can hunt so many species, and if you
wanted to, you could hunt the whole year—deer and bear and
moose in fall, bobcat and grouse in December, coyote in January
and February, and rabbit in March, take April off and hunt turkey
in May and June, then back to coyote again until August when bear
season begins anew.

Fall is the season that matters most. Moose, deer, and bear
comprise Maine's big three game species. Coyotes, unknown in
Maine as recently as thirty years ago, are now populous. Raccoons,
skunks, and porcupines have always enjoyed a home here. Be

sure to check the hunting rules and regulations before you hunt any animal! You cannot, for example, hunt a fisher cat or a pine marten. Wild turkey have flourished since being introduced some years ago. Fox have always been here as well.

Pheasant, ruffed grouse, bobwhite quail, and woodcock offer upland bird hunters a wonderful wing season. The rest of the year

offers plenty of action. Bobcat hunting in the dead of winter is considered by many to be Maine's most challenging hunt, and I can testify to that. Spend a lot of time in the gym before you go. And did I mention crows and squirrels, red and gray?

Some two hundred thousand hunters take to the field in Maine annually. About fourteen percent of the population hunts, one of the largest percentages in the nation.

For me, hunting is about solitude and camaraderie both. I enjoy the solitude of being alone in the woods and the companionship of friends back at camp.

I've had many special moments in the woods with the most memorable being, when I ran into legendary whitetail hunter Larry Benoit of Vermont. I am not going to tell you where I met him, but it was very close to one of the public lands mentioned in this book.

Another time I had a rabbit run between my legs as he ran for his life, trying to avoid the murderous intentions of a fisher cat.

And of course I have been lost.

And found.

I have hunted in rain and snow and temperatures so low the NOAA radio advised against going out of doors.

I've hunted early in the morning, late in the evening, and all hours in between. I've hunted with a bow and arrow and a shotgun and a high-powered rifle and a .22 pistol.

I've made some life-long friends along the way.

Benoit famously said "a sportsman can be judged by his manners." So true. And by that standard, the vast majority of hunters I have met in the field in Maine are decent, kind folk.

So no matter what you choose to pursue in the woods of Maine, I'm sure you'll have a good time.

BE SAFE!

5. THE FAMOUS MAINE MOOSE

Maine is home to a large moose population. The hunt was resurrected in 1980 and is conducted through a lottery system. It's a very popular hunt, often referred to as the "hunt of a lifetime." There are some very fine trophy bulls to be had, and those who opt to shoot cows can be assured of a freezer full of some wonderful meat.

Of late, many of the "road moose" that were once so plentiful seem to have smartened up, and hunters have to take to the woods more to find their prize. Also, a lot of the open woods that afforded good moose sightings have grown up over the last twenty-seven years, and that, along with a ban on clearcutting, has made the big critter less visible. This has bred a number of expert moose callers, who use a variety of horns, old coffee cans, and their own vocalizations to lure in a trophy animal.

Non-residents are allowed to enter the lottery as well as residents, and I encourage you to do so.

It's a great hunt.

6. BEAR HUNT

Bear hunting remains a prominent sport in northern Maine. A healthy population of bruins totals some twenty-three thousand animals. Bear trapping is also permitted by law in Maine, as well as the use of dogs in pursuing the animal.

I prefer to hunt bears with dogs. Hunters are allowed to use two dogs at a time, and the hounds are amazing in their ability to track down a bear and tree it or hold it at bay. It's a very successful method and far less static than hunting over bait or trapping.

My friend Sonny Wade and his protégé Buzz Mendoza have been hunting bears for years and during that time taken many dozens of bears. Buzz has more than ten hounds, and some of his "strikers" are considered amongst the finest in the country. The day I

W. K. Thorndike

W.K. Thorndike

hunted with Sonny and Buzz was a fine, sunny, almost summer-like day. The dogs had a bear at bay, and as we hiked into the woods we could hear the excited yelps and barks of the dogs.

There are few things in life like coming up a knoll and seeing the dogs with a big black bear at bay. When the bear spotted us, it sprinted to a tree and was up it in a flash. After we tied up the dogs I shot the bear, and it came tumbling to the ground, a nice three-hundred-pound sow.

Maine is gifted with some superb taxidermists, and I took my bear to Art Fayta in Pownal, a true master. My bear will make a magnificent rug.

There are many talented bear hunters in Maine, and any eager bruin killer will not have to look too far to find one.

7. DOGS

The North Woods and Maine's public lands are a paradise for dogs—hunting dogs and pointers and bear dogs and Rover the house pet. I swear my dogs know when I am going upcountry, because they howl and shriek when I take out the blaze-orange vests they wear during hunting season. One of them is such a hard charger I had to buy a chest protector to keep her front end from being torn to pieces.

I had another dog that was a terrific swimmer. Lots of opportunities there for the aquatic canine. She would swim no matter what the temperature; the only thing that stopped her was when the ponds froze over.

So by all means bring your pooch. If you hunt woodcock, you need a dog for sure. Hunting bear with dogs is major fun, but you must have a Maine guide accompany you if you are "from away." Even coyotes are hunted with dogs in Maine. So too are rabbit and grouse. So there is a big mix of dogs and game.

Unfortunately, I know of cases where beagles have been attacked and killed by (a) a mountain lion, (b) a coyote, or (c) a wolf. This while hunting rabbits. My own dog has been attacked by coyotes and has the bite marks on her hindquarters to prove it. So if your dog is off the leash and not under voice control, beware.

My favorite dog of all time was wonderful in the woods, dutifully heeling all the way. She was not a terribly game dog. But she loved being in the woods, except in the rain. My other dog would go out in a blizzard and be more than happy.

So don't forget Rover when you come to Maine. Every sporting camp I know welcomes pets.

8. TRACKING BOBCATS DOWNEAST

The bobcat dashes through the woods in regal silence. The hounds give chase, baying and barking. It's January in the Maine woods, and it's so cold my coffee froze while I was drinking it.

I am with Paul Laney, Maine's premier houndsman. We are hunting public land Downeast. The hunt costs not a dime, and there is no one around to disturb us.

We chase the dogs chasing the cat. I am huffing and puffing, and my lungs are ready to burst. My heart rate is—I don't want to know. Laney is tall and lithe, and I am not.

The cat flashes by me in a blur with the dogs in hot pursuit. I am hesitant to shoot. No dog is worth shooting with a poorly placed shot at the bobcat.

I must wait.

Paul remains hot on the track, but I am running out of steam and have to pause to recover. I am inhaling giant buckets of cold air. My legs are leaden. My shotgun weighs a ton.

Onward!

Now I am following Paul's snowshoe prints. My own webs are clacking together in a noisy cacophony of wood on wood. I hear the hounds change pitch. They have the cat at bay.

"Hurry!" shouts Paul.

Minutes later I arrive on the scene, and the cat is hissing and spitting. The dogs keep the cat in place; there is nowhere for him to escape. It is a big tomcat. Paul hands me the .22 pistol.

"Shoot him!"

I take careful aim but cannot get a shot without a dog in the way.

"Careful!"

Seconds pass, and I line up a clean shot. I pull the trigger. The cat collapses and the report dies out in the deep woods.

The dogs pounce.

"Let them enjoy their kill," says Laney. "They worked hard for it."

The dogs maul the cat savagely.

It is almost dark, and we pull the dogs off the kill and make our way back to the truck. We are in a mile from the truck, hunting the public preserve in Cutler. Everything is tinted blue by the moon.

Back at the truck I turn the heat on high and marvel at the beauty of the woods. Magically, I hear the ocean crashing around us. The surf rolling to shore. That's how close we are to the beach.

The next day we are up well before dawn. Coffee and eggs and bacon make a good breakfast. It will be many hours till we enjoy another hot meal.

The temperature this day is twenty below. The wind is out of the north at 10 mph and gusting to 20 mph. The NOAA radio strongly suggests we stay inside. Laney rolls his eyes.

"Staying inside is not an option," he says, smiling.

Once more we venture out, driving slowly, slowly looking for cat tracks where they crossed the tote road the night before. The track reminds me of a seashell, delicate and deeply articulated.

"Bingo," says Paul. He stops the Chevy Silverado and gets out to inspect the track.

"Small one," he says. "Let's keep looking."

Two hours later we find a track Paul likes. It is big and makes a deep impression in the snow. Many trackers mistake fisher and coyote for bobcat, but Paul relies on years and years of experience.

The ritual begins all over again. We cover all exposed flesh and arm ourselves with marine band radios. I take my shotgun in case we tree a cat.

The dogs are let out and immediately get on the scent of the cat. If they chase the bobcat hard, the cat will begin to sweat, and the scent will grow stronger. The snow is deep this year—three feet or so—and the cat will need to leap through it.

The cat will tire.

The dogs will not.

This time the hunt is mercifully short. The cat is treed by the dogs in less than one hour.

This time Paul does not exhort me to hurry; the cat is not going anywhere. When I arrive on the scene and shoot it, it falls gracelessly into the soft snow.

"Very nice tom," he says.

Indeed. The cat later tips the scales at almost forty pounds.

There is absolutely no one around to share the moment but Paul and I. We make our way out to the road and once more crank the heater to high.

The third day of our hunt we end up on the beach, and the cat runs into the ledges, and we lose the advantage the dogs have in heavy cover. The cat holes up in the rocks, and we cannot get it.

The dogs are disappointed, milling about and trying to understand how the cat can elude them.

One more adventure on Maine's public lands. There is much to cover in our quest for a record-book cat. Because in Maine today there are one million acres of public lands.

9. GOSHAWK STRIKE

The bird watching in Maine is fabulous. Eagles abound, in southern and northern Maine. Osprey are all around the rivers and lakes and streams. Along the Cutler Coast there is plenty of bald eagle action, and nothing compares to the majesty of a full, mature bald eagle.

But my most memorable bird event was near the Day's Academy

Grant, part of the million acres of public land owned by the State of Maine. I was hunting grouse with my wife, Lisa, and I spotted one run into the undergrowth.

"I'm going after that bird," I said.

I flushed it twice, and the second time it flew into the top of a gray birch tree. I raised my gun. But before I could pull the trigger, a goshawk swept down and hit that poor grouse so hard I thought it would explode.

After a moment, during which we were drop-jawed with amazement, the big bird of prey flapped its wings heavy and hard and flew off, grouse in its talons.

I don't expect much will top that in my lifetime.

Lesser thrills still remain constant in memory. One very tame encounter in the woods is with the American bittern, a bird that seems so friendly and relaxed that you could reach out and take him home with you.

My love for predators is well fed in Maine. Hawks alone tally at least five well-known birds. Broad-winged, Cooper's, red-shouldered, red-tailed, sharp-shinned, all reside here in Maine, as well as northern harriers, goshawks, nighthawks, and peregrine falcons. All of them are protected by law, as are songbirds.

Ducks abound, and some of them are among the prettiest birds on the planet, and here I am referring to the wood duck and my favorite, the harlequin duck. I am also partial to mergansers, both the hooded variety and the red-breasted variety.

I'm told the pileated woodpecker is the model for Woody the Woodpecker. You sure can hear it a long way off. It is a big bird and sports a bright red cap and moustache. A really fun bird to see, and its size always surprises.

I've never seen a whip-poor-will, but brother, I have spent many a sleepless night listening to one! Whether you sleep through it or not depends. But it is something to experience, as it never, ever, shuts up.

In fall, when I am running the roads for grouse, juncos fly ahead of the truck from mile to mile, and when the snow flies, the snow buntings appear.

Two more very large birds are the great blue heron and the osprey or sea eagle. They are seen throughout the state, and the heron lumbers on takeoff. The osprey fishes all the time and soars high over the ocean and rivers.

I don't know if you have ever seen a killdeer feign injury, but I have and it's a scream. The bird does a great ham actor impression of trying to maneuver with a broken wing. It does this to draw predators from its nest, and once the job is done, it takes to the wing.

My favorite owl is the barred owl, because I can talk to it by using a call and the phrase, "Who cooks for you?" It's so much fun to hear them respond. And then there is the great horned owl, which has eyes like a human and the nickname "flying tiger" because it takes on skunks and porcupines.

There are many excellent field guides available at most bookstores, and it's a great way to introduce yourself to birding in Maine.

10. SHED HUNT

It is May 16th in northern Maine. The temperature is 33 degrees. The wind is out of the north at 10 mph with gusts to 20 mph. It is snowing hard.

I am freezing.

But if there is such a thing as "good freezing," this is it. I am hard on the track of dropped antlers in the Day's Academy Grant.

I am hunting for what are known in Maine as "sheds." These are the antlers dropped by moose and deer deep in midwinter. Now that the snow has melted (more or less), I am in the woods, deep in the woods, prowling a moose yard.

There is more moose scat than I have ever seen in one place, and my expectations are high. But as in any kind of hunting, nothing is guaranteed. I walk with my eyes swiveling right to left and hard ahead.

An old skidder road has given way to a well-trampled game path, and I know from all the sign that moose are here—and were here. I spot a dead animal, most likely frozen to death during the hard winter, and two live animals hoofing through the thick brush effortlessly. Their long legs carry them over the blowdowns and slash effortlessly.

Hours go by, and I spy two deer, a partridge, and an eagle overhead. This is my moose "honey hole," and I have collected some nice sheds here before.

I find moose hair and striped maple, stripped of its bark, a favorite food for moose, but no sheds. Patience is a hunting virtue, I remind myself and keep on walking. Slowly I cover ground. Even if I do not find a shed, the woods are waking after the long winter, and the trees are starting to leaf out.

And then it happens.

I have entered a wet, grassy marsh, and on the edge of it I find the best horn I have ever found. It is large and still "in the brown." That

W. K. Thorndike

means it was shed in this winter and has yet to be bleached white by the sun. It is much as it was when it crowned the head of a large bull.

I do not pick it up at first; I simply stop and wonder at the magic of it all. It has ten points and has not been gnawed at by porcupines or squirrels. I approach closer and lift it up. It is heavy with big "spoons" or what some refer to as the "palms" of the antler. Large and flat bone that gives a moose its majestic appearance.

It is heavy as I lug it out of the woods, probably fifteen pounds or so, but I carry it with glee. A souvenir that will last me the rest of my life.

The rest of the day I court hypothermia. I have forgotten to bring a change of clothing and mark my mind not to do that again. The day passes, and I am wet to the skin, but the trophy antler sustains me.

I keep looking.

At three o'clock on a day that began before sunrise, I quit. Few shed hunts end with such good luck. I am ready for another hunt, on another day.

The million acres of public land stretch out before me as one long, drop zone. Hunters find sheds and so do snowmobilers. But this time of year, when the snow is melted, is the sweetest time to look for sheds.

Many times I have taken out friends and acquaintances who do not approve of hunting and introduced them to the fine art of finding sheds. Nobody gets hurt, no animals get killed, and yet the hunt is as exciting as any I've been on.

I drive back to Greenville, and when I stop for gas the driver of the car next to me looks in the back of my pickup truck and gasps. "That's some horn!" he says.

And it's mine, I think. I found it, and it's mine to keep forever.

If you are interested in shed hunting, try to find a place where moose are known to yard up for the winter, and the same applies to deer. If you find a nice one, keep looking. Moose and deer often drop their antlers in close proximity to one another. Keep looking and you just might find its mate.

No matter how you approach shed hunting, it makes for a

memorable spring outing, trophies or not. The bugs are just around the bend, and this is the time to enjoy the woods before you need a gallon of bug juice. Most of all, mark your favorite spot, because moose and deer tend to yard up in the same place year after year. With some practice and some exploring, you will be able to return year after year for sheds.

And you'll soon have your own list of honey holes. And plenty of souvenirs for your friends to admire. You'll have spent nothing on bullets, and if you hunt Maine's public lands, it won't cost you a penny.

Note: A year later Lee Schanz and I go back and snag seven excellent moose horn sheds in a single day. The weather was perfect!

11. ON PA'TRIDGE

Maine offers some of the world's finest ruffed grouse hunting. In Maine the birds are known colloquially as "pa'tridge." A friend of mine said when God created pa'tridge he did a "mighty fine paint job." Indeed, the birds are spectacular in their plumage. Some are in a dark phase, while others are in a cinnamon phase. In good years they seem to be everywhere, and in bad years they seem to be nowhere. This season was hard to describe. Some hunters had very good luck and others less so. I suppose it illustrates the old maxim that the birds are "where you find them."

Some folks hunt birds from their truck in an attempt to pick off road birds pecking at the gravel; some folks use dogs. Still others take to the woods and hunt the birds there. Another old Maine maxim applies here. "They all taste the same in the frying pan."

And they are wonderfully good eating. As with a lot of fine meals, superior fresh ingredients make a simple meal unforgettable. I breast out the bird and cut the breast into strips and sauté it in a frying pan with butter and salt and pepper. That's it, your recipe for grouse supreme.

You are allowed to shoot four birds a day, and the possession limit is eight bids. A 20-gauge shotgun is the weapon of choice.

Hunting hours are from half an hour before sunrise to half an hour after sunset. I prefer to brine the birds in saltwater for twenty-four hours before cooking. Softens them up and gets rid of any lingering gaminess, though eating them without brining is preferred by many. The meat is lean and tasty and tender. Serve with crescent rolls and baked beans and beer or wine or my favorite, champagne.

Season runs through December 31st.

12. ALLAGASH LAKE

Allagash Lake lies in the heart of my favorite part of Maine. It's some seventy miles from Kokadjo, and even in hunting season it's quiet. On a recent visit in October, I ran the roads for birds without seeing a soul. If solitude is something you are after—and who isn't in today's multi-technology world?—then visiting Maine's public lands is an invaluable escape.

The walk in to the lake was a moderately long one, and let me assure you, the odds that you are going to meet someone in the woods itself during such a walk in October are virtually nil. I expected to see moose and I did, a large bull in regal isolation. Moose, as I discuss in the chapter on moose, are not as readily apparent as they once were, due in part to their intelligence and the fact that so many clearcuts are now grown tall.

The temperature this fine October day was near seventy, and the leaves were at the peak of their splendor. I left in the early morning with my pack and a sandwich, a bottle of water, and high hopes of finding a buck rub. I use the bird season as an early buck scouting opportunity as well as the chance to eat pa'tridge.

I started coming upcountry years ago, and not much has changed. There are still loggers and hunters and fishermen and camps. There are more road signs than before but still plenty of unmarked roads, too. When I got to the shore of the lake and realized there was no easy motorized access, I felt happy. Maine has the last great wilderness tract on the East Coast of America. Already there is talk of development and more houses, resorts, etc. So I seize each day as a chance to enjoy the woods before the paving trucks come. All the more reason to memorize each and every tract of public land, which will escape development forever.

The lake glimmers like a mirror.

When I walk back I sit by a stack of newly cut hemlock and inhale the sweet aroma like it was fine pipe tobacco. I eat my sandwich and recognize that all food tastes better in the out-of-doors. My water tastes cool and fresh. The sunshine beats down on me with a comforting warmth. The sky is a deep blue. Such are the attributes of a northern Maine excursion.

This is a great part of the state from which to branch out and explore fine wilderness. There is the entire Allagash Wilderness Waterway, one of Maine's most famous waterways and one of the most beautiful spots on the planet.

Nearby Chamberlain Lake, Eagle Lake, Indian Lake, and Round Pond all offer classic Maine settings—fir forest, clear water, mountain views, and lots of game. In my opinion, this is the best place in the state to go exploring public lands.

13. THE RIGHT FIREARMS

Ah, guns. Mainers love guns and have a lot of them and of all kinds, shotguns and rifles and pistols. I think that's why the crime rate is so low, because would-be miscreants know grandma is probably sitting on the couch watching TV with a .30-30 beside her.

But as the old saying goes, "Beware a man who owns only one gun, because he may know how to use it." I have a friend who calls himself a "gun minimalist." He owns one rifle, one pistol, and one shotgun. That's it.

So with that in mind, let me recommend to you how to assemble a small number of firearms—four—that will enable you to hunt everything there is to hunt in the Maine woods. Buy these guns used, and you'll save a big pile of money.

A good shotgun can be used for everything from coyote to rabbit and grouse. I recommend a 12-gauge as an all-round-gauge gun, but if you plan to hunt grouse exclusively, I suggest picking up a 20-gauge because it doesn't pepper the grouse as much as a 12 does. If possible, get an over-and-under or a classic side-by-side, because they are more reliable and more maintenance free than a semi-auto.

If you really want an upland gun, then take a page from the Maine chapter of the North American Versatile Hunting Dog Association and buy a nice 20-gauge and cut the barrels down to 20 inches. Have the barrel backbored. Leave the choke at cylinder bore and install silver welded studs and sling swivels. Now you have a gun you can carry all day in the woods and which works fine on pa'tridge.

Now for a pistol. Best all-round pistol is a .22, and with that you can kill almost anything but a bear, a moose, or a deer. It's real good for rabbits and bobcats. Works for grouse too, and squirrels. I own a Ruger semi-auto. There's a ton of them around, and if you want you can buy a revolver. Plus, this gun is great fun for plinking, and you can do a lot of that on the public lands, and safely. Ammo is cheap as well.

Now for rifles.

My primary rifle is a Remington 7600 in carbine length. Caliber .30-06. Pump action. Normally known as a "Benoit-style rifle" after the famous Vermont hunting family. I install a Williams peep sight and take the reticle out to make a ghost ring. I also employ a Williams sight on front, a so-called fire sight. Very useful in low-light conditions. Lately, the Benoits have taken to using a Trijicon scope, so you might want to check that out. They call it a "tri-con."

Now anything you don't understand about what I've just written down, that's OK. You shouldn't. Take it to a good gunsmith, and he'll be happy to tell you what I mean. That's because it needs to be SHOWN to you, and I can't do that in a book.

This is a brush gun designed for the dense growth of the Maine woods and allows for rapid follow-up shots if needed. It's a fabulous deer gun but is also effective on bear. It's also a big-time fun gun and deadly accurate up to 100 yards.

My other rifle has a Burris scope on it. It's a Model 77 MK II Ruger, also in .30-06. Why? Because everyone—most especially older deer hunters—needs a gun with a good scope on it. It really brings the target in closer and allows a more accurate shot for most shooters. I use a 4x fixed because I think that's all that is necessary.

You can add to your collection as you want because, like most of us, we have every gun we need but not every gun we want.

Remember, safety is paramount when it comes to guns. They are extremely unforgiving of sloppy handling. Remember, any game you are pursuing is not worth an accident, and always know what you are shooting at and what's behind it before you pull the trigger.

That's a wonderful thing about the Maine public lands, in that they afford a safe place to shoot.

Shoot to have some fun, but also shoot safely, and you'll have years of good shooting times ahead of you.

14. PREPAREDNESS

The Boy Scouts have it right.

BE PREPARED

The wilderness sites I visited in the course of preparing this guide are challenging even to the most masterful woodsman. For a neophyte, an unprepared visit can be disastrous.

Solo visits require the most vigilance of all.

Do not go into the woods alone unless you are competent with a compass! This is the single greatest source of woods trouble. Getting lost in the big woods is frightening and potentially deadly.

Many "newbies" rely too much on the state-of-the-art Global Positioning System. Batteries can and do fail. GPSs can be dropped and lost (I know, it has happened to me). In short, any mechanical device can fail.

A compass is nearly unbreakable, and if you carry two, the odds of your making it out of the woods are high. Of course, no compass can tell you where you are if you have not taken a bearing before you venture out.

Be prepared. I take a lot of ribbing about the pack I carry, loaded to the gunwales with survival equipment, but I feel confident I am prepared to deal with nearly any mishap.

The basic rule of thumb I use is to be prepared to spend the night in the woods. It will likely happen to you at some point. Nighttime navigation in the big woods is not something anyone should engage in, unless you are a Maine game warden or a master Maine guide intent on rescuing a lost hunter, hiker, or fisherman. Make sure you start your way out by midafternoon.

If you are not familiar with using a compass (and you would be amazed how many people today are not) you MUST LEARN HOW!

The compass "bible" is titled, *Be Expert with Map & Compass* by Björn Kjellström. Buy it.

Another very good rule of thumb is to practice with everything you will take with you into the woods in your backyard first. This means everything from your Coleman lantern to your tent and stove. The initial trip into the woods is NOT the time to see how everything sets up and works (or not).

A map seems such an afterthought that I mention it only because it seems so obvious. Topo maps are easy to read even for a beginner. You must learn to link the compass to the map. If you do, you will be on your way to becoming a woodsman. If you do not, you are skating on thin ice (another Maine hazard).

Here's a ritual I make use of every time I leave my truck and head into the deep woods. I look around me and make sure I take into account every major landmark (mountains, fire towers, rivers, streams, roads) so that I have the most basic means of navigation—by sight. Major landmarks do not move!

I then orient myself with my compass. This is a simple but highly effective way to make sure you come out in good shape. If my compass points to the way I am going to walk in, reversing the way will bring me out! If I fail to do this before I head into the woods, no manner of compass computing will show me the way out.

If you are with a companion, have him or her do the same. If you are traveling with small children, I recommend you do not go into the deep woods whatsoever. Help is far away when you are in the wilderness.

Take at least two spare tires. The logging roads in Maine are sharp with shale and other rocks, and flats are a way of life. I just recently encountered a couple who had three flats in one trip.

So let's go through my pack. I think that will best illustrate what it takes to make a wilderness trip safely. It's too late when you say, "I wish I had brought my flashlight" to illuminate your way around the campground at dark. Life in the woods is of course a fun time, and a little humor doesn't hurt anyone. I've written before about what to take in your pack, but inevitably the first thing people scream about if I leave it out is TOILET PAPER. Enough said.

I haul my dunnage in a glorified fanny pack of good quality. It's heavy, and that's why most people don't like to take such a life-saving kit. I've been lost many times and hurt seriously once when deep in the woods, so I don't mind. Neither will you if trouble comes your way. A compass, a knife, and some matches do not cut it. Maybe that was enough for Daniel Boone, but I wager if

Mr. Boone had access to our modern devices, he'd grab at them happily.

Here we go:
PERSONAL LOCATOR BEACON
WATER
FLASHLIGHT
KNIFE
SATELLITE PHONE
TWO GPS
TWO COMPASSES
HUNTING AND FISHING LICENSE
EXTRA BATTERIES
FIRE STARTER + MAINE BEAN CAN
HEADLAMP
SPACE BLANKET
TOILET PAPER
SIGNAL MIRROR
SURVEYOR'S TAPE
BUG DOPE
DISPOSABLE CAMERA
MATCHES
LEATHERMAN
SMALL COIL OF ROPE

The Maine bean can is very handy in starting a fire. Even in the rain, a fire can be started in the can, and then sticks can be placed over it. Essential.

I recommend a SureFire flashlight as they are very bright and very rugged.

A PLB (personal locator beacon) is a must for those traveling alone in the woods. This satellite device calls for help in the case of a bona fide emergency. They are pricey but worth it ten times over if you break a leg—or worse—in the woods and are unable to continue your trip out.

Water. Well, you cannot take enough of it! Same goes for bug dope.

Surveyor's tape is helpful if you need to mark an important site (where your prized buck lies).

A satellite phone is also pricey but most helpful in the many areas of northern Maine where a cell phone is useless. Another invaluable emergency tool.

The Leatherman multi-tool has saved my bacon a million times.

If you get a space blanket, get it in the sleeping-bag configuration.

There you have it. Everyone has their preferences, of course, but these are mine. ANY BIT OF SURVIVAL EQUIPMENT IS BETTER THAN NONE!

If you are too timid to go it alone, or smart enough to know your skills are not advanced enough for deep woods adventures, HIRE A MAINE GUIDE. That's what they do for a living.

It's always a good idea to let someone know of your plans. I call my wife every night on my satellite phone to let her know I'm OK after a day in the woods.

The very best base camp is a Maine sporting camp. The Maine Sporting Camp Association has a Web site and lists all the camps. I highly recommend Libby's, Red River Camps, Nahmakanta and Spencer Pond camps.

A good sleeping bag and rain gear are also MUSTS. If you are tenting, again, put the tent up in the backyard and sleep in it overnight. NOT WHEN YOU GET TO THE WOODS!

A shovel and a good base for a jack—a stout piece of plywood—will help you if you have tire problems or get stuck in snow or mud.

I do not mean to frighten you out of a wilderness trip but only to apprise you of the risks. They are manageable risks IF YOU PLAN FOR THEM.

I've seen too many unprepared people in the woods to not emphasize how very important it is to BE PREPARED.

I cannot sum up years of experience and hundreds of days in the field in this short a space. Just keep in mind that a wilderness area is not your local park, and you'll be OK. If you do take the necessary precautions, you'll enjoy your trip to the fullest.

15. THE LEGEND OF THE NORTH MAINE WOODS

My favorite North Maine Woods memory of all time took place some ten years ago in a location I will never divulge, only to say, yes, it was very near to a public land. I go there often still.

It was deer season. Cool, clear, and crisp. Late morning. I had gone into a very thick patch of woods and was tired of fighting for every inch of ground. I came out of the woods and onto a tote road. Anyone who has left the big thick woods for the comforts of a tote road knows what I am talking about. I relished the easy walking.

To my considerable annoyance, a truck came along. It had Vermont plates. They read, CCC BOY.

Now the Civilian Conservation Corps goes back a way, and I am not sure there are a lot of people who remember the Roosevelt era social program anymore. But I did and was mildly intrigued, if still annoyed that someone had broken my silent reverie.

The truck stopped, and the man behind the wheel rolled down the window. An older man with long hair.

"Were you really in the CCC?" I asked.

"I sure was," he said.

He had on that green plaid all the Vermont deer hunters wear, a Johnson hunting jacket. Everyone who hunts deer anywhere in New England knows about the Benoits, the legendary hunting family from Duxbury, so I asked the obvious question. "You know the Benoits?"

"Sure do."

"How old is the old man now, 75?"

"76."

"How do you know," I asked, a tad churlish.

"Because you're looking at him."

Well. The world stopped spinning for a moment.

"You are Larry Benoit?" I stammered.

"I am."

I had stumbled on Larry Benoit, the world's most famous deer hunter. I looked at him and yes, the long hair, the steely eyes, the Vermont accented voice . . . great Caesar's ghost!

Then I saw his rifle, a Remington pump-gun carbine, and I knew I was in the presence of greatness.

And the world stopped spinning for a moment. Again.

Since that time I got to know Larry better, and my life has been richer for it. So you see, you never know just what might happen if you tramp through the woods in the north of Maine.

You might even meet your hero.

16. FISH ON THE FLY

Brook trout are tasty. And they taste even better if you catch one with a fly rod.

Don't be intimidated by the fact that so many fly-fishing men and women are consummate devotees of the sport and have spent years honing their skills.

It's just not that difficult.

And it's just not that easy.

But it sure is fun to learn.

A good rod and reel and line can be had for less than $150. Throw in some flies and a leader, and you are still under $160. Not too bad.

If you know an experienced fly fisher, a few lessons are the best way to go. But let me cover some of the basics for you.

A fly rod swing is always from 10 o'clock to 2 o'clock. At first, practice on your lawn. And leave the fly off the line; this comes later. Make sure on your back cast you let the line run straight out before you cast forward. Practice casting back and forth, letting the line play out as you go back and forth. This is called "false casting."

Make certain you hold the excess line taut on the back swing. Practice letting a little more line out each time. The line should stretch out and lie down nice and straight (easier said than done, but you have to start somewhere!).

Do this 10,000 times.

Now try it with a fly attached. And several feet of leader.

Repeat 10,000 times.

A good fly fisher can introduce these skills quickly enough, in an hour or so, for you to begin practicing on your own. When you see an accomplished angler cast expertly, trust me, there has been one heck of a lot of practice.

Then go to a dock that allows for plenty of back cast and start laying the line on water. How this is different from casting on the lawn is beyond me, but it is. The water seems to do magical and demonical things to the line. And now, you are truly fishing, aiming at a brook trout!

Did I mention how very tasty brook trout are, fried in a pan with lots of butter?

Your next step is to get out on the pond or stream you are going to fish. Bring a net.

Keep practicing your cast—you will never stop practicing, ever—and lay the line quietly and gently and perfectly straight out on the water. Sooner than later you will in all likelihood catch a fish. I did the first time I went onto open water with my handy fly rod. Learn to tie a barrel knot and a fisherman's knot. They are not terribly difficult. You use the first to link one line of a lesser diameter to another line. As in: your leader to your line. Never say string!

17. SPRING AT DEBOULLIE

The cutting stopped at the borderline of the Deboullie public land. The slash heaps and ravaged landscape—all of a sudden—were gone, and in its place was an unmolested Maine forest. I was entering a northern paradise, home to the most exceptional fishing waters in the state and some of the most picturesque campsites in Maine.

"No cutting." Ah, what a beautiful pair of words! All around me was virgin forest. And plenty of it. Deboullie measures 21,871 acres. You could take weeks to tour it and not take it all in.

And the quiet! I strained my ears for the sounds of a saw or a generator or a skidder, and all around me there was nothing but silence. It was like stepping into the past. No phones, no computers, no fax machines. No pagers, beepers, or cell phones!

Paradise.

A ring-necked duck swam by and then a goldeneye. Loons glided by in regal plumage. A fly fisherman stood at the dock of the place I was staying at—Red River Camps—and I was transfixed by the gentle arc of the line and the soft lapping sound it made when it hit the water. The bugs were still few in number—this was just prior to Memorial Day weekend—and I did not care a whit.

Yessir, no bugs was fine with me. The temperature was in the mid 70s, and the sky was blue and cloudless. All around me the sky bordered dark growth, so that the forest seemed to end in a clear, ragged line.

I took out a book and pulled up a chair and read till sunset. Mike Brophy, the owner of the camp and a longtime resident of the Deboullie unit, stopped by and asked me what I had in mind.

"You tell me," I said.

"Try climbing Deboullie Mountain," he replied. "There's a beautiful campsite at the base of the mountain and a fire tower up top. You can climb the fire tower and see all around for miles and miles."

I feasted on a solid supper of beef stew and biscuits and

pumpkin pie before retiring. I was in an old log cabin, underneath a wool blanket. I left the door open and heard a hummingbird on its final foray of the evening.

In the morning the breakfast bell rang and I scampered out of the sack. A big breakfast and off I went. Feeling a bit like a daredevil, I drove through the Red River right where it is born at the outlet from Pushineer Pond.

The truck skidded on big, smooth riverbed rocks. It was not a terribly difficult crossing, but it gave me a dose of adrenalin.

There was a campsite on the other side, and it was pristine and unoccupied. I ran into a Department of Conservation employee, Ranger Arnold Martin, and we laughed about reveling in the last days before the bugs arrived.

"Sweetest time of the year," he said. Seemed he was interested in spending the day outside as well.

I set off on the well-marked trail. No one about. Not too long into the hike I ran into the Deboullie unit's namesake: a giant rockslide lay before me. It was as if there was a mammoth jetty all around me.

I walked across the base of the rockslide as if it were a massive playground, hopping from boulder to boulder. How long had it been there? I decided it was a very, very long time. Long enough, surely, for the French colonists to name it "tumbledown."

A blue moth flew past me. The color of a robin's egg. Now, I must find out what that moth is, I thought. And then I thought, why bother? It's a blue moth, and that's enough to know. A blue moth as delicate and wonderful as a bluebird.

The Deboullie campsite, at the base of the mountain of the same name, is on the water and shaded by the forest. Nobody home.

I begin my ascent with some trepidation. The climb is, in places, just short of technical climbing. In other words, a rope and some carabiners would probably come in handy. But I stumble into a cluster of purple trillium, and I marvel at the wildflowers. They are just blooming. I find some old telephone wire leading up to the fire tower and the old fire ranger's cabin. I keep climbing. I have more than 1,800 feet to go, most of it almost straight uphill. I

pause often. But finally the summit is in sight, and when I crest the mountain I am rewarded with a vista that is a perfect summation of the Maine forest. Water is all around me.

I am too cowardly to climb the fire tower; it seems a foolhardy

gesture in light of the fact I am all alone. Mike Brophy assures me it is perfectly safe and one of the few fire towers made safe by the Department of Conservation rather than scuttled. But I pass. Let some more intrepid visitors make the final ascent!

I return to camp after four hours of steady climbing (mind you, the climb down is just as nerve-wracking and treacherous as the way up) and eat a dinner of pork parmesan and pasta.

Gary Corson, one of the camp's fishing guides, regales me with tales of rare blueback trout and wild brook trout and the famous Black Pond.

"Best fishing in the state," he says. "No question."

I am to return with my rod. And by the way, this is fly-fishing only.

The cost of my romp through Deboullie?

Nothing.

It's all public land. If you camp at the campsite and bring your own grub, it won't cost you a nickel. A gate fee applies in some areas, to get you to the public lands, and Red River Camps are modestly expensive, but for the true roughing-it aficionado, it doesn't come any cheaper—or any better—than the Deboullie unit, property of the State of Maine.

18. DOWNEAST

I decided to revisit some of the old places I had visited, and some new ones, in the fall of 2007. I began with Day's Academy and the public parcel around Lobster Mountain. The first of October saw great weather and lots of foliage. The leaves were muted in their colors, a little bit washed out, because of a drought. I marveled at the most basic treasure—no houses and no telephone wires and no paved roads.

A man approached me on the road I was walking, as I was hunting partridge, and asked me for directions to Little Spencer Mountain. I had to laugh. Little Spencer Mountain can be seen for many miles around. But he was seeking the path that leads to the summit, and perhaps I was being a little superior. I hopped in his car and took him to his destination and shot two birds on the way.

"You live in paradise!" the man exclaimed. He was from New

York. "I hope you appreciate it."

Well, I do.

My favorite thing in the whole world to do is hunt partridge. The birds this year were not plentiful, but they were not scarce either. We would ride the roads and walk the woods and come home with enough birds to make a splendid dinner. The secret to any good meal is fresh ingredients, and nothing is fresher than a bird you just killed. All it takes is a skillet, some butter and salt and pepper, and you are in business. The meat is wonderfully lean and tasty.

The bird can be wily. Some fly to safety and others run away through the forest, never to be found. Still others hide in the brush and are never seen in the first place. Dogs are used to hunt them, too, but any hunter can pursue them on foot and do well, if patient. And then there is hunting from a truck, a delightful and comfortable way to hunt, running the logging roads that run on forever.

I like to spend the entire day outside, and in October I can hunt in a t-shirt. For all the color that paints the landscape, there remain considerable amounts of green, and I know in the weeks to come the hunting will be better. The birds will not be able to conceal themselves as easily.

From Day's Academy I head down east, with some serious driving ahead of me. I leave Whitefield in the morning, and five hours later I am at Cutler and the Bold Coast Trails.

I don't see the ocean at first, but I hear it coming through the damp pine and fir forest. I hear a grouse drumming, but today I am a hiker, not a hunter. The trailhead is right off Route 191. The parking lot is full. I see one couple with a young boy. It's a very special kind of hike, because very few hikes begin in deep woods and end up with a spectacular, ocean view.

Downeast is magical. The ocean is everywhere, and the sunrise and sunsets are magnificent. I stay ocean-side to watch the sun set in a fiery blaze of orange and yellow and red. My thoughts are of the last days up north, with the delights of bird hunting, and I shake my head to think I am somewhat wistful. As if this view wasn't enough for a man!

The following day I travel further on into the heart of Downeast—Grand Lake Stream. I am headed for Duck Lake. I stop at the village store, the capital of the town, and ask for directions. I am given detailed instruction. I bring out my gazetteer and pencil the route out to Duck. The counterman is also a guide, and we laugh when we try to guess how many Duck Lakes there are in Maine.

I travel a dozen miles and kill three partridge on the way. I am a happy man. I pass a few other hunters and a coyote trapper. I pass through the Unknown Lakes, the sound of which still amuses me. At the Duck campsite there is no one, and the sense of solitude is profound. I yell out loud, and all that I hear coming back is the echo off the lake.

I hike around the lake and bag two more birds. Plenty for a nice big bird feed for three.

I remember talking to a game warden and his reaction to his first day on the job. "Lonely out there when you're alone," he said.

It sure is. It took me a long time to accustom myself to being all alone in the woods but once I did, well, it's addictive. I try to prepare myself for all contingencies and I am not foolish, but when you are alone there is nobody to help you. It builds character. I navigate by gazetteer until I see a sign for the Unknowns and Duck Lake and realize I am on Indian property. But soon I am back on public land, and I am happy to think this part of the woods will stay the same in perpetuity. Just as the Indians once knew it!

I pitch my tent and listen to the stillness and eat some of the grouse and lie back and look at the stars, the sky big and clear and crisp. It's hard to believe the campsite is deserted. Such perfect weather. It rained hard the day before, and the ground is still damp, but the temperature is in the high 40s, and come daytime it will reach into the 50s. Good sleeping weather and a fabulous sunrise.

I pass back through the Unknowns and half expect to be swept up by ghosts but make it safely back to the road to Grand Lake.

The next day I am off to Donnell Pond, near Cherryfield. I drive along a ten-mile scenic stretch of road that is fall foliage at its best. I pull over to take some photos, and other than the traffic, there is no one around. The boat launch is empty, and all that remains are summer memories. I am reminded of how rich Maine is in lakes and ponds, all of them achingly beautiful. Donnell Pond is twisted and cut with peninsulas, and as I drive around it, I see it from a different perspective every hundred yards or so.

I've traveled some five hundred miles since leaving Whitefield. At each location, Cutler, Duck Lake, and Donnell Pond, I could have taken weeks to explore the countryside. It's that big a territory. Maine is a big, big place, and my gas bill proves it. I've chosen to travel at the height of the foliage explosion, and everywhere I go the color is vibrant and rich.

Now it is time to head north again.

19. STAYING FOUND

Getting found and staying found is the primary goal of any North Woods adventurer. It's a big territory, and you need always keep that in mind. Put it this way: a game warden I know covers a district the size of Connecticut.

The primary way to find yourself is the DeLorme Gazetteer. Every year the atlas is updated. Roads change and change and change again in northern Maine, and not every map is entirely accurate or complete. But the gazetteer is a fine map, regardless, and no one who knows the woods is without one. Be advised.

When you buy one—and they are sold almost everywhere—buy a highlighter pen and the plastic cover that helps keep the maps from being destroyed. I suggest you buy two so that you and your co-navigator don't have to bend over and pore over the same map. It's a big help.

But before I go into some of the details of getting found and staying found, let me post some basic laws of North Woods navigation.

1. Never, ever, ever fail to ask for help in finding your way. Swallow your pride and admit to the

obvious, that you need some help. I start with the following phrase: "Can you help me?" Commit it to memory. Mainers are famously friendly and eager to help. Be assured that they will immediately turn to their gazetteer, so that's just another reason for you to have yours.

2. Do your primary exploration early in the day. When I have a big mission, I start at dawn. I feel a whole lot more confident when I have all day ahead of me. Trying to navigate at night is a major mistake. A bit of advice you must take heed of for safety reasons that are obvious—it is very, very hard to see a moose at night.

3. Buy a GPS and learn how to use it. Christopher Columbus would have killed for one. It is one of the great inventions of the twentieth century. The TrackBack feature alone is worth the cost, and good ones are available for $100. I prefer the Garmin brand.

4. Never underestimate the continuing merits of a good topo map. If you know how to use UTM, it is really useful. Don't know what UTM is? Buy a GPS.

5. When in doubt, back out. Tote roads in Maine turn to you-know-what pretty quick, and when they do, reconsider all notions of plowing ahead. I carry a whole assortment of stuff in case I get stuck. See #6.

6. Two extra spares. Saw. Winch. Axe. Fix-a-Flat. Chain saw. Sturdy jack (not the one that comes with the truck). Hubcap wrench, also from an auto-parts store. Come-along. Front hitch. And this list is endless!

7. Did I say truck? I see more and more cars on the tote roads, but I think it is pure foolishness. A good truck means four-wheel drive and an extra low gear. That extra low gear has saved me so many times. Good sturdy tires are also a must. I recommend the B.F. Goodrich All-Terrain T/A KO. Most flat tires are caused by sharp rocks that pierce the sidewall. I have had tires shredded to pieces by the slate that is used to make roads. One spare is simply not enough. I have had three flat tires at a time. EXTRA GASOLINE! The nearest gas station can be many, many miles away.

8. Stay way out of the way of logging trucks. When I see one coming I pull over (and I mean OVER) and say a prayer. Navigation means nothing if you don't survive to make the trip. This can be a very humbling experience for the uninitiated.

9. Here is a simple rule I use over and over and over again, and you should have it tattooed on your hand. When you get out of your vehicle and are ready to get going, use the sound of the door slamming shut as a cue. Familiarize yourself with the landscape and make note of any major landmarks (mountains for example). Take a good look at your compass and note the direction of the road. Whatever direction you take TAKE A BACK BEARING!!! This is simple. If the direction you head is north, your back bearing is south. YOUR BACK BEARING TAKES YOU BACK HOME!!! I see more people go off into the woods without a clue as to where they are headed, and then they wonder why they get lost.

10. If you do not use a compass and know how to use it correctly, you have NO BUSINESS in the woods. Buy a copy of *Be Expert with Map & Compass* by Björn Kjellström. I repeat this, I know, but it's worth repeating! It's the compass bible. The Boy Scout handbook works pretty well, too. I am amazed at how few people really know how to use a compass. It never fails, it needs no batteries, and it never wears out. A compass does you no good if you do not look at it BEFORE you get going. These may sound like simple notions, but trust me, they are profound in their import.

11. Take a GPS waypoint as often as you can. You can never have enough waypoints. Waypoints let you know where you have been and where to go to GO BACK!

12. In the chapter on preparedness, I wrote about the importance of having the right gear and that neatly dovetails with this chapter. Anything that detracts from your main mission—navigation—is a nuisance and takes away from your main goal. Wet feet and cold hands are good examples.

OK back to the beginning.

Let's say I want to go to Allagash Lake. I examine the map and determine there is no way to drive directly to the lake shore. But

I find one path (PATH!) that leads me pretty close to the water. I first must make sure I locate the same path as I am looking at on the map.

The one I see is off the Narrow Pond Road—very close to the boat landing at Narrow Pond—and goes very straight north to south. I use the scale on the map and decide it is a couple of miles to the lake.

I try a few paths that do not go straight until I am sure this is the one. It's the closest to the boat landing, but I want to make damned sure I am right. I go to a local camp and ASK! But guess what? They are not sure. So now I am on my own.

I take my pack and note the time, so I know how long it will take me to come back to the truck. I look at landmarks (Narrow Pond). I make a waypoint and take a compass bearing and a back bearing. Now, I am ready.

Remember to take water and toilet paper.

And indeed, after a couple of miles of walking what amounts to a moose path—I am there! Hooray!

Don't let anyone make fun of you for being so purposeful and thorough. It's like gun safety—you can never have enough of it.

A lot of road systems in Maine woods are not connected. That means one road will end before another begins and that either of them goes to a different place. Sound confusing? You bet!

Now, I don't want to frighten anyone off from exploring the woods. I just want you to be safe. Getting lost in the woods can be TERRIFYING. So let's talk about getting lost, because it will happen sooner or later.

If nothing else, pick a straight line to walk, and this is where your compass will help you, even if you did nothing else right. Don't walk in circles. Look for a stream. It will flow downstream somewhere bigger and perhaps to a camp.

DO NOT PANIC. If you feel yourself panicking, remember you are prepared to spend the night, and after all you are not on Mt. Everest. Stop and smoke a cigarette or have a cup of coffee. Assess. Did you tell someone where you were? Oftenmost, I am alone and no one knows exactly where I am. You may find yourself in the same spot. In most places these days, you are not more than a mile or two from a road. That should comfort you. If you have a gun you can signal for help. (Three shots spaced out should be answered with one).

DO NOT keep going in the dark; it's time to go to bed.

Same thing applies if you get lost on a tote road. You should bed down and wait till morning, and you can spend the time poring over your gazetteer.

You don't get good at navigating in the woods without practice. Nobody comes out of the womb with a compass around their neck. BE NOT AFRAID!

I repeat. Time in the woods, most especially time alone, can be daunting. There is a marvelous book called *Lost! on a Mountain in Maine* by Donn Fendler that recounts the true adventures of a lost boy in the woods. Fear rides on the wings of solitude! As I wrote in the chapter on being alone, true solitude is unfamiliar territory in our world today. Trust nature to guide you above everything else. You'll learn a lot about yourself, believe me.

Again, don't ever succumb to being too proud to ask for directions! Going into the big woods is not a day trip to the local park and should never be treated as such. Prepare for it, and you'll be able to enjoy its magic safely and happily. Bring the kids!

20. NAHMAKANTA

My visit to Nahmakanta began with a funeral service in New York City. The city's calamity of noise and furious activity had left me ragged and jittery. An old friend was dead. It was time to go home to Maine.

Time to go to Nahmakanta.

I wasn't sure what I would find in the giant wilderness tract. The now public land totals more than forty-four thousand acres. Part of the Appalachian Trail runs through it. And the Debsconeag Lakes region, in the northeast corner of the parcel, is Maine's largest ecological reserve.

In Greenville, I filled my truck up with gasoline. There are no gas stations where I was headed. I stopped at a fishing store and bought some fresh leader and some new flies. The weather was perfect. Sunny skies and temperatures in the 70s as the calendar closed in on the summer solstice. I was traveling on a weekday, and the roads were largely deserted.

I passed no one—not a single soul—on my way in to Nahmakanta. The Indian word means "shimmering pond with many jumping fish." But twice I stopped my truck to gaze upon a woodcock mother with her brood and a partridge mother with her brood. The baby birds were a mere three inches tall.

My spirits lifted.

I also encountered a cow moose. I stopped my truck and turned off the engine. The moose stared at me without moving. I whistled and the moose perked up its ears. I suppose we stayed there staring at one another for a good three minutes.

Now New York was a memory, and the present reality—a deserted woods road in northern Maine—was quiet and still. Only the gentle wind rustling the leaves made a sound. And the birds. I heard a pileated woodpecker ring out and watched an eagle soar above me. When people ask me what is so special about Maine, I tell them it is the nothingness that is so wonderful and profound.

And that's if nothing means no buildings, no highways, no supermarkets, and no cell-phone towers. No . . . thing. How badly I wanted to experience nothing, instead of something. To be a part of the natural world, without the increasingly endless stimulus of the techno-modern society we live in. Simply put, I was looking for some good old-fashioned peace and quiet.

I made my way slowly and delightfully to Nahmakanta Lake Wilderness Camps, run by Don and Angel Hibbs. Their young daughter, Freddy, pranced across a well-tended lawn. All the camps faced the lake. Don came out to greet me and escort me to my cabin. I was reminded of how lucky I was to be there.

Nahmakanta offers some fine fishing, and other guests were busy trying to hook salmon and trout. I sat on the porch and soaked it all up—the nothingness. The water and the sun and the horizon, all in perfect harmony. I sat there till supper was served in an old-time lodge. The other guests were flush with the delights of fishing and sipping red wine as the light on the lake glowed yellow and gold.

I watched them go back out again after the meal, and as dusk settled, the lake became pockmarked with fish rising to the surface to feed. I practiced my fly-casting and floated in a canoe in a state of bliss. No noise, no distractions, no blaring sirens or horns. I'd brought a novel by the famed Japanese novelist Haruki Murakami, and sitting there reading it I thought, this is the cure for what ails me. Our modern life is so deeply non-spiritual, and human existence is all about spirituality. My church, my religion, it's the great outdoors. It's impossible to experience the big Maine woods and not feel that there is something bigger than all of us out there. And the feeling is comforting. Who could stare at the sunset over the lake and not feel pleased?

In the morning I ate a huge breakfast, cooked up by Angel and delivered to the table by Freddy, and planned my day. I thought I would trek the Appalachian Trail, since I'd never been on it

before. It ran along Rainbow Stream where I planned to intercept it. Rainbow Stream. Rainbow Township. I thought about how beautiful a rainbow trout is. A fish that glows in your hand, a palette of gentle colors. Less than twenty-four hours into my trip and already I felt a palpable sense of relaxation. As if every muscle in my body was loosening and softening. I picked up my pack and my compass and headed out.

For four hours I roamed north and south on the famous trail and encountered . . . no one.

The stream gurgled. It rushed over rocks and flowed vigorously downstream and never stopped. I stopped many times and sat on the bank and felt completely whole. And I reminded myself that with the threat of development rearing its ugly head in northern Maine, this land was public land and would stay that way.

This and almost a million other acres of woods, all for people like me. Open to all traditional uses. If the rest are as likeable as Nahmakanta, then I had a lot of traveling ahead of me. Knowing they would be there, unchanged, forever, thrilled me.

Rain fell.

I made my way to Crescent Pond and heard the rain make its way through the woods, spattering the leaves with clean, fresh water and stippling the stream with raindrops. I came back to camp and got back into my truck and drove around the lake, past a boat launch, and encountered more moose. I saw bear sign and laughed. For there is no mistaking bear sign.

The next day the sun returned, and I found an old skidder path and hiked it for three hours before I ran out of energy and turned around and made my way back to camp. Where did that path end? It seemed a rhetorical question. And what did I see?

Nothing.

Nothing but woods.

That night, after another super supper, I sat on the porch and gazed over the setting sun and sighed. An old friend was dead. But I was alive, very much alive, in Nahmakanta.

21. EXTREME COLD

I remember the coldest day I've experienced in Maine, and it was years ago on top of Saddleback Mountain. The chalkboard next to the ski lift said sixty-nine below with the wind chill factored in. In addition it said: "No exposed flesh allowed."

I should hope not!

I've hunted bobcats with Paul Laney in January and have gone out on days when NOAA weather radio says not to go outside. I am not joking. We're talking twenty-nine below on the thermometer, not to mention wind speed. Let me tell you what this kind of cold will do. If you take off your mitten (mittens work better than gloves in this cold, because there is no space between the fingers for the cold to intrude) your fingers will freeze solid in a very, very short time. Then you have a very serious problem, like losing your fingers.

I do not exaggerate.

So if you go up to the woods in the depth of winter, make sure you have the cold-weather gear you need to survive. I mean pac boots, serious headgear, a generous parka and wool pants, long johns and mittens, and I don't mean the kind of mittens your mother gives you for Christmas. North Face makes great cold-weather gear.

Make sure you bring water and have some way to keep it from freezing solid. Carry it on your person. You'll need it even if you don't feel thirsty. You burn a lot of calories in very cold weather.

And never go alone.

22. LISTS AND MORE LISTS

If you are like everyone else in America, packing for a trip usually requires the services of an eighteen-wheeler. We're a nation of excess, and seldom is that excess expressed so clearly as when a family tries to pack to go camping.

I think a great way to cut down on your dunnage is to take everything on a trip and then make a careful list of what you did NOT use and what you did NOT really need and discard those things on your next trip.

Every trip you make you will take less stuff.

And if you go on enough trips, you'll have a list of stuff to take, and that list will be a good thin one. There's a kind of epiphany when that happens, because it is liberating. I started off with everything but the kitchen sink. Today, well, I am not perfect, but the stuff I bring is considerably less.

Lists are essential and save you the trouble of starting all over the next time you take a woods trip. I keep mine on my computer,

so I can easily add and subtract items as I wish. Every year I make changes, but fewer than ever before.

Always keep a flashlight in your vehicle. It sounds obvious, but when it gets dark and you don't have any light, well—

I use one that I can put around my head, so I have both hands free. It's a great device.

When we go to camp, we always bring a lot of food, because at camp eating well is a given. Coolers are necessary. They make some great ones today. When the food is gone, you can use the cooler for packing space for other things. The space that food takes up is considerable, but when we leave the food is gone and voilà! We have more space than before we left.

Tupperware containers are best for avoiding water damage from rain and snow. They come in a variety of sizes and are easy to carry back and forth from the truck to the cabin.

Tie-downs also are a good idea, to secure your load.

Rain gear is, as it always has been, the first thing you can lay your hands on, and toilet paper. I also make sure I have some snacks in the cab, some good stuff to make the trip more . . . palatable. Smoked salmon and cheddar cheese and Wheat Thins are a favorite combo.

And don't forget your woods pack that has all the things you need to go tromping in the woods. That way you can hike some trails before you get to camp and not have to go digging for your compass and knife.

Count on forgetting something and don't sweat it when you do. Life is too short. Making a list helps to eliminate this problem, but not completely. I just accept it as a fact of life.

23. SNOWSHOES

My old friend Gene Letourneau called them "the webs," but we all know them as snowshoes. "Floats" is another old Maine term. Both nicknames do them more justice than the proper name.

I have a small collection of Tubbs, Iversons, and L.L.Bean webs.

Some are aluminum and plastic, but I prefer the old-fashioned ash and leather construction, though most webs today are made of neoprene.

It's a misconception that snowshoes carry you above the snow. You still sink in, unless you are on a groomed, hard-packed trail like one made for snowmobiles or cross-country skiing. The real purpose of snowshoes is to keep you from sinking entirely in deep snow. Now I am talking about snow above your knees and deeper. In that instance, snowshoes allow you to go where it would otherwise prove impossible. The results are different depending on the type of snow, wet and heavy versus light and fluffy, for example, but you'll be able to "float" high enough above the snowpack to make your way forward.

Everything changes completely when you get off a groomed trail and into the woods. Now the shoes are trying to make their way past the tangle of limbs and sticks and detritus that makes up the Maine forest floor. It would probably make sense now to skip to the chapter on falling.

This is a real skill. If you are not careful, the shoes can "bridge" and break. The frame of the shoe rides atop two logs, say, and when you step forward the weight is too great and crack!

Falling on snowshoes is a tricky business. You fall in a great heap into deep snow, and righting yourself is a different order of magnitude than doing so on bare ground. It's quite hilarious at times, like an elephant trying to get up from a bed of deep sand. I hate it. The problem is getting the snowshoes underneath you, so you can stand straight up.

Try it!

Another problem occurs on the opposite end of the scale, and that's getting the shoes on in the first place. Skinny, fit people do well, as they do at almost anything involving manual dexterity, but if you are overweight or clumsy, watch out. Bending over to tie up the straps that hold the shoe to your foot can be a bit of a chore, especially in cold weather with gloves or mittens on.

Enormous improvements have been made in the harnesses used to anchor your feet to the shoe. I'd still like to see something more akin to the bindings used on skis, but then I have a tendency

to complain about snowshoes in general because they can be bulky
and awkward.

   All of this can be easily avoided, however, by taking to the trails

used by snowmobiles and cross-country skiers. You can really fly on these trails. The aerobic workout is nothing compared to the lung-busting paroxysms of deep-snow antics, but the fun factor is a lot greater.

Make sure you have enough shoe. Lots of folks like bear paws, almost round shoes of large diameter, but I'm not convinced they work well for larger folks. Larger shoes mean more flotation surface, and aluminum shoes have a plastic decking that surpasses webbing by a mile, because it is solid and not webbed.

If you plan on getting a solid workout from your shoes, go easy on your dress. You'll easily overheat. Dress as you would if you were cross-country skiing. And if you are in the woods for any length of time, make sure you carry a replacement strap for your binding. This can be a real lifesaver.

If you have really old-style shoes with catgut webbing, you need to lacquer them from time to time to help preserve the wood and the webbing. It doesn't take too much effort, and you ensure the well-being of the shoes for more years to come.

Besides, snowshoes look really cool hanging on the wall of your den, next to your rifle.

24. FOUL WEATHER

Good weather is a good thing in the North Maine Woods. But it's not always that way, of course, and you need to prepare for rain, sleet and snow, ice, fog, and wind. I've been in bad weather in all the seasons of the calendar.

On my trip Downeast it poured buckets. I had some good rain gear and waterproof boots, so off I went and had a ball. You meet other folks out in the bad weather too. The trail to the ocean at Cutler Coast had some dozen or so hikers that day. It was warm, which helped, but then if it had been much cooler it could have been snow.

Tenting is a tough regimen but still a lot of fun. I guess you could say you know nothing about tenting until you tent in the rain.

That's when you learn about ditching a moat around your tent and how effective a rain fly really is. I'm not going to get into a long discourse on tenting, but one of the most fun things to do in the woods is walk really far into the woods and pitch your tent for the night. The night in the woods is full of sounds and stars and is truly something magical.

A tent also ensures that if you get lost you can almost laugh it off, because you have brought shelter with you and can begin your search to get found all over again in the morning.

Snow is another matter. October usually features snow at some point in the month, and while recent Novembers have been warm and relatively snow free, heavy snow and frigid temperatures are always a possibility. Snowshoes are not out of the question in November, and if you muzzle-loader hunt, then they are even more of a possibility. I take two sets of clothing for the fall, one moderately heavy and the other genuinely heavy—wool jacket and long underwear and heavy boots.

The worse the weather gets, the better the chance you will slip and fall in the woods. All of which reinforces the importance of being prepared for an emergency.

25. FALLING

When someone tells me they never fall in the woods or, for that matter, never get lost, I tell them they haven't spent very much time in the woods!

Navigating the big woods means stepping over and under blowdowns, crossing slash piles, climbing ridges and coming back down, crossing streams, swimming through oceans of raspberry bushes, and stepping over boulder-strewn byways.

Let me put it to you this way. I carry a rifle made largely of indestructible plastic. I can drop it and it won't even leave a dent. I did this after wrecking several good wooden stocks and fore-ends. I guess I fall about two or three times a hunting season and about that proportionally the rest of the year. And this is after years

and years of learning how to walk through the woods without falling.

I suffered one disastrous fall. That was when I was hunting outside lower Hudson way upcountry and fell and broke three ribs. I tried to hurdle a big blowdown, and instead of going over it, I fell backwards and onto my back.

Ouch!

It's always best to think two or three steps ahead, much like a billiards player who is thinking two or three shots ahead of the shot at hand. You must watch your step very, very carefully, most especially when traversing a big field of slash. Honestly, I dread slash piles.

Another important rule is never to step on a log. Why? Because they often break, or worse, are wicked slippery. Step over! Whenever you can, step on solid ground. And if you do fall, try to let go and accept the fact you are going down. Less chance of injury this way.

If I weren't carrying a rifle or a shotgun, I might carry a walking stick. If you are merely hiking, why not? I think it's a great way to help stabilize yourself in rugged terrain.

A word about climbing. While there are no truly technical climbs in most woods adventures, there are some genuine mountains and some very pronounced inclines. And not that going up is the only risk—there is coming down, which to my mind is equally risky. If you are alone, be extra careful. I climbed Deboullie Mountain by myself and can still remember the steep pitch. And the descent. My wife says these climbs should NOT be attempted alone, and I have to say she is probably right.

Fire towers provide glorious vistas but are not for the faint hearted. These structures are usually in fair condition, but still, be extra careful, and do not climb one alone. Frankly, they are pretty hairy.

If you are a hunter, practice walking without breaking or snapping any twigs. This is wonderful experience for hunting deer. If you are a deer tracker and there is good tracking snow, remember to keep your eyes not only on the tracks but on the woods around you. Too many hunters forget to look around them and concentrate on the track to the exclusion of everything else!

Finally, a word about eye injuries. They are very common in the woods and serious. With all the brush to penetrate, you WILL get something poking you in the eye sooner or later. Do your best to protect yourself. I have sometimes pondered the use of a motorcycle helmet. When I must push through a thicket, I keep my eyes down and my hands over them. I'll walk blindly for a couple of steps, open my eyes, and repeat.

Once, while hunting bobcat with Paul Laney, who has lost dozens of contact lenses in the woods, I stumbled and almost put my eye out on a stub on a dead pine tree. Another quarter inch and the stub would have been in my eye. You can't prevent everything from happening. But be conscious of your eyes; as Mother said, you only have two of them.

Make sure you follow basic procedures when walking with others and keep your distance from the person ahead of you. Watch those whips! This is a sure way to get hurt. What's the rush, right? I always keep a healthy distance between myself and the person ahead of me.

Hypothermia is a killer and must be taken very, very seriously. If your teeth start to chatter, you are in the first phase of hypothermia, or if you are shivering uncontrollably, watch out. Stop and build a fire and warm up. Immediately! And keep in mind that hypothermia can occur at a 55-degree temperature. Wet weather with a little wind and you'll cool down rapidly and maybe dangerously.

Make sure you dress appropriately. It's better to shed some clothing than wish to add on and not have any. Be particularly careful about rain and rain gear. Number-one rule: if you are wet in the woods, you will never have much fun, and you may be endangering yourself.

It is not my intention to scare you. But there are hazards in the woods, and the best thing to fight them is to be aware of them and act accordingly.

26. ON READING AND TV

Some years ago I gave up watching television. And it all came about from staying at camp, where almost always there is no TV.

I rediscovered reading. Some years I read twenty books during the fall at camp. When the hunting day is over at four o'clock, and it's dark, there is more than enough time to dig in and read a big book. I can tear through a book in a few days, and the continuity of a read like that is not to be matched by reading a book over a period of weeks, or months. My wife, whom I call the "human chainsaw," can rip through a book in one day! Some people play cards to pass the time, some listen to music. At Spencer Pond I have heard a guest playing the violin. Lots of folks shoot the breeze until bedtime, which is the second most preferable way to pass the time, if you ask me. Especially with people you don't know; there is so much to talk about with a stranger.

I still went to the length of disconnecting my TV at home from its cable box. I think TV is a bit of an addictive drug, the "video drug," as it is sometimes known, and there's no use having the temptation around. But it doesn't bother me as much as it used to; in fact it doesn't bother me at all. The house is quieter, much quieter; a reflection of the quiet in the woods, and my mind is stiller, like it is in the woods. I don't spend all that time in front of the boob tube and have found all sorts of thing to do in that time I've gained.

W.K.Thorndike

The reading that has the greatest application in the woods is field manuals, and I own a ton of them. Birds, mammals, tracks, butterflies, and insects, flowers, and scat, they all help make a better woodsman. There is nothing you cannot learn from a book, and field manuals are graphic evidence of that rule. I use them all the time.

27. SCRAPES AND OTHER IMPORTANT MATTERS

If you are not a deer hunter, you might want to acquaint yourself with the signs of mating season, because it is one time when the animals leave obvious signs of their presence and their desire to mate. Perhaps you have seen these signs in the woods and not known what they are.

The first sign is called a "scrape." This occurs when a buck uses his hooves to scrape a bald patch on the forest floor and then urinate on it to signal he is ready to mate and looking for a partner.

Big bucks make big scrapes. Some are territorial and some are purely for mating purposes. In a forest full of fallen leaves, scrapes are pretty hard to miss. A scrape assures you that a buck is in the vicinity.

A rub is the result of a buck rubbing his antlers against a small tree, a sapling or a fir tree. Rubs are usually from two to four feet off the ground. The bark of the tree will be rubbed clean and strips of bark will hang from the rub like string. The bigger the rub, the bigger the buck, because bigger antlers make bigger marks on the tree. Sometimes the rubs extend in a line, and that too can give you a clue as to the size of the buck, depending on the amount of ruckus he has caused as he walks his rub line.

There are not a lot of deer in northern Maine, but the ones that do live there are big and can often exceed two hundred pounds in weight. That is why hunters like to hunt in Maine, in the hopes that they can bag a monster buck.

As for moose. Moose are plentiful in Maine. They are primarily docile animals, and huge. It is possible to get close to moose, but one should always keep in mind that moose are wild animals and capable of charging when annoyed. Like deer, moose rub trees and make scrapes, although their efforts are higher on the tree and broader on the ground. Moose like to use their teeth to strip the bark off trees, most notably striped maple, and when they are present in an area the trees are all marked and torn up.

Moose tracks are very large and easy to identify. They are similar to deer tracks, only three times the size. Moose also cause deadly car collisions, and driving at night in northern Maine requires careful maneuvering. On tote roads, moose can appear quite suddenly from the brush on the side of the road. Be careful!

Another warning that bears repeating. An additional road hazard is man made, and that is the presence almost everywhere in the North Woods of logging trucks, enormous in size and prone to high rates of speed. The first rule when dealing with logging trucks is to YIELD. This means pull over to the shoulder at the first sighting of a truck. This means pull over as far as you can. When approaching bridges, make short shrift of crossing the bridge. You don't want to be stuck on a bridge when a big truck approaches. This is serious business and should be taken that way.

In snow these dangers are magnified, and driving should be left to someone who has experience in these conditions. WINTER IS NOT THE TIME TO LEARN HOW TO DRIVE ON MAINE'S LOGGING ROADS!

At other times, working crews will be using the road to load logs. You must stop and let them finish their business before proceeding. Turn on the radio and relax; it can take 30 minutes for them to finish before allowing you to pass. Trying to pass when they are working is very poor form and dangerous to boot.

Never block off a road. This too is very poor form. And if you encounter another vehicle on a narrow road/path, do your best to allow them to pass. As Larry Benoit once observed, you can tell a good woodsman by their manners. This is another maxim that bears endless repeating.

28. WOODS CHURCH

I don't know what your religion is, or denomination. And I don't really care. One of my favorite sayings is that "religion is for people who want to go to heaven, and spirituality is for people who have been to hell." Whatever. I just want to let you know what the woods have done for me in terms of how I feel about God.

Only God could have made the woods and its creatures.

Only God could have invented snow and water and trees, the sky and the moon and the sun.

Only God could make clouds and the wind and light and dark.

Only God could make the quiet of a calm, summer day and the crashing, impossibly loud noise of a thunderstorm.

Spend some time in the Maine woods, and you'll know what I am talking about. There is nothing manmade about it. They are big and grand and achingly beautiful. They are always in flux, changing from a cold spring to a warm summer to a crisp fall to a frigid winter. No two days ever the same.

So much of the joy of the Maine woods is how removed it is from the high-tech society we live in. You needn't a fax or a computer or a pager or a cell phone or a palm pilot. You just don't need those things. Manmade things.

There are fewer and fewer places left to watch a starry night in all its regal glory, but the Maine woods remains one. God surely made the stars. I love to lie on my back and stargaze. You can see the universe move. Top that.

I don't know why it is, but when I am in the woods, I spend a lot of time thinking about the temporary nature of existence. Maybe it is because I spend a lot of time in the woods during the four seasons. Life and death is as much a part of the woods as life and death is on a farm. There is birth and growth and death. The entire life cycle is represented over and over again.

I see people in cities, and they are all on the phone. I wonder, what is so important? There seems to be a fear of quietude. But in the woods there is nothing but quiet (OK, OK, I know, there is a lot of woodcutting and attendant noises), at least a goodly part of the time, and you can hear yourself think.

And in that quiet you can hear the voice of the Creator.

I see people come to the Maine woods for the first time, and more and more of them are staying at traditional Maine hunting and fishing camps. So things are changing. They come from Boston and New York to recover from the stresses of the big cities. They come to get some taste of God's natural world, to reflect. And whether they know it or not, they are entering a place where God's handiwork is readily apparent.

It just couldn't have all happened by accident; I don't know anyone who thinks that.

In the modern times, maybe we think we are the commander of all things. But in the woods, I feel small and inconsequential. And I don't mean this in a bad way. I just recognize that I am a small part of the natural world, far smaller than being only one person amongst billions here on planet Earth.

And I believe when I die that I will return here as some part of nature, even if my dust simply becomes part of the soil, because so much springs from the soil. Maybe I will be a tree.

Just one more reason to be thankful there are a million acres of public land in Maine, to go to, and just . . . be.

29. HUNT TELOS FOREVER

I am up before dawn, and the temperature is 14 degrees with snow, perfect deer-hunting weather. The dark gives way to a steely gray morning, and by first light I am far into the woods, in pursuit of a trophy whitetail.

I see no one. I have already scouted the area where I am hunting, a parcel of land known as Telos, part of the million acres of public land in Maine that is open to traditional uses.

Hunting is one of them.

I make my way around a giant cedar bog, looking for tracks. A dusting of snow blankets the landscape like a gentle white hand. The air is crisp, clean and cold, and my breath comes out as steam. The day finally breaks out into full light, and I begin a long trek up the side of a mountain.

My hunt is costing me nothing, and I am on one of the premier hunting grounds in America for trophy whitetail deer, animals of two hundred pounds plus.

I do not find a big buck track, but I do find some doe tracks, and it follows that where the does are the bucks cannot be far behind. My lungs start to get a workout as I climb up and up towards the big bucks' favorite environs, the high ridges.

In an era when the fate of the North Woods is unknown and change is the order of the day, Maine's public lands offer a respite from the constant shifting of ownership of large parcels of forest. The public parcels are also free of large-scale timbering.

"We like to see people take advantage of these public lands, because that is precisely what they are there for," says Maine Department of Conservation Commissioner Patrick McGowan. "It doesn't matter what the pursuit is, hunting, fishing, snowmobiling, snowshoeing, hiking, camping, canoeing. What does matter is that the State wants to keep land open for these activities at no cost to the users."

And that includes out-of-staters.

By mid-morning I have been outdoors for five hours and stop

for a snack of raisins and nuts and chocolate chips. I need my energy to keep chasing deer all day long. Not too long after I am done snacking, I jump a beautiful eight-pointer.

And he is gone in a flash.

I begin the long and unpredictable pursuit; the big buck's prints large enough to accommodate a 30.06 rifle cartridge. I wade through thick pine groves and past beaver flowages. An osprey glides overhead. When I slow down to a crawl, hoping I am near the buck, a fisher spies me and spends several seconds checking me out before scampering back into the thick brush.

By noon a bright sun has broken through the clouds, and the temperature climbs 10 degrees. I continue to cover ground, walking a game trail and pushing my way past a thousand branches and blowdowns. This is not an easy hunt and is not territory for the uninitiated. A solid grasp of the elements of woods navigation is critically important. A GPS device is mighty handy, too, in woods that seemingly go on forever.

But it is the remoteness that characterizes what Maine wilderness has to offer, and I am blissfully alone. The solitude also makes for very safe hunting—I am unlikely to run into another hunter. At noon I stop for a genuine woods meal—peanut butter and jelly sandwich and water from my canteen—and put down my rifle.

I am high up again, looking for that old buck that likes to run ridges. He keeps me trekking along the ridgeline, and the tracks are fresh. By three o'clock I am dead tired, and the sun is starting to set, and I ask myself where the day went.

The next day I start out before dawn again and do not get back to my camp until dark. I spend the entire day out in the woods looking for my trophy buck. Nothing makes me happier.

What makes Telos special, and the million acres of Maine public land, is that it is unchanging permanence, and I can come back again and again to hunt or fish or snowmobile. So can my children. It's comforting to know that in a world of change, this parcel of land will remain forever wild.

A lot of visitors to Maine have their favorite spots, and now they can count public lands among those places. The best part, perhaps, is that the public lands are free for the exploring.

For a map of Maine's public lands, check out the Maine Department of Conservation online.

30. SPRING ARRIVES

Winter dies hard in northern Maine.

Three to four feet of snow lies in the forest. The trees are still bare, even on the first day of spring, and temperatures routinely fall to the single digits at night. But the long winter is finally starting to come to a close.

I am in search of rabbits, and the beagles are howling. My snowshoes are not necessary in the morning, but completely necessary by afternoon. The rabbits are so white I have to look for a pair of pink eyes to spot my prey.

"Go anywhere during the morning, go nowhere in the afternoon," jokes my hunting partner Jim McMullen. He is only half kidding.

We did not have to ask permission to hunt here because we are back on Maine public land—this enormous parcel known as Telos—some fifty miles outside of Ashland. There are only sporting camps here and there and no electricity, no stores, no parking lots, and no hassles.

In short, a hunter's paradise.

It's as close to an undisturbed wilderness as anyplace left. We spend all day hunting rabbits, bagging four nice snowshoe hare, and we never see another soul. By the way, cottontail rabbits are illegal to hunt and are listed now as endangered. But rabbits are mostly residents of southern Maine, endangered or not.

Welcome again to just one piece of public land in Maine, part of a million acres of wild land where a person can hunt or fish for free, without asking permission, and for as long as we like.

We traveled a long way from Ashland on the paper-company road known as the Pinkham Road before hitting the Telos Road and the abutting hunting ground—hundreds and hundreds of acres of pines and hardwoods. The roads are similar to the woods, easy going when frozen and a muddy mess when the sun melts the icy tundra. I am giddy with delight at being alone, and I get out of the truck and take a potshot at a fast-moving coyote.

A coyote faster than I am on the trigger.

Even Mainers are mostly unaware of the abundance of public lands, and with the North Woods changing rapidly, public land becomes a more valuable asset for hunters and fishermen every year. These are lands held in perpetuity, and nearly all of them are earmarked for traditional uses.

Later that day we put on our shoes and walk along a game trail, looking for an eagle nest. We had spotted the giant bird in the sky above us and thought we might get lucky and find its nest. No luck, but we got a good workout tramping through the woods on the webs. Eagles have long been protected in Maine and successfully so, having been removed from the endangered species list not too long ago. There are signs of spring. The chickadees are singing and the coltsfoot is near to sprouting. The days are longer, and at night the sound of coyote pups can be heard, earnest and juvenile. The ice is almost out on the ponds and lakes. It is near to the opening of fishing season.

This is a precious time in the North Woods, because the black flies and no-see-ums are not out yet. Soon there will be days of bright sunshine and blue skies, when the weather outmatches the dull gray tones of the forest, and the sky loses its battleship-gray contours. The winter parkas will soon be too warm to wear, and the sun will burn skin red for the fair-skinned out all day long.

"A lot of folks like to complain about paying taxes, but this is one area where their taxes go to something they can enjoy for nothing," notes Commissioner McGowan. "We've worked hard to secure these lands and make them available to the public to hike, snowshoe, snowmobile, picnic, hunt and fish. We want people to know they are welcome year round to enjoy them."

On a starry night I set up my sleeping bag over a bed of pine-tree boughs and revel in the universe. It's an overwhelming feeling. City dwellers might have forgotten what a star-filled night sky may be like, but up here it is almost taken for granted.

In the distance I hear a bull moose bellowing. An owl hooting.

And a bird I cannot identify. I try to memorize its song, so I can ask a bird biologist what it might be when I get back to Augusta.

For the next month or so I can enjoy the woods bug free and fee free! There is no limit on how long I can camp in the woods and no prohibition on hunting. And I know that if I want to come back, I can do so year after year, each year getting to know the Telos ground better, and it will always be waiting for me.

Never changing.

Canadian jays fly to me as I enjoy a lunchtime snack of saltines, peanut butter, and chocolate chips. The air is cool and redolent of pine. I spend my last day following a bobcat track and looking for moose and deer sheds.

Just as I am about the leave the woods, I spot the brown tip of a moose antler jutting out at an awkward angle from a patch of shallow snow.

Eureka!

And with that lifetime souvenir, I am headed back to Ashland and civilization, already anticipating my return to these lands.

Afterword

I traveled several thousand miles writing this guide to Maine's public lands. It was exhilarating. I made trips in all four seasons and never enjoyed myself more. I close my eyes, and I see places like Nahmakanta and Deboullie and Allagash Lake and am transported to the most beautiful spots in all of Maine.

And that is saying something.

In a time when every inch of earth is being paved over, Maine's public lands offer a permanent and unchanging place to go and experience the glory of Mother Nature. More will be added with time. It's all part of Mainers' making sure the nature of our state remains steadfast.

Voters have passed referenda time and time again approving millions of dollars for acquisition of new lands. There is a genuine sentiment to protect what we have, the last great forest on the east coast of the United States.

My thanks to the commissioner of the Maine Department of Conservation, Patrick K. McGowan, for assigning me the journalistic task of a lifetime.

TOM HANRAHAN is one of Maine's most renowned outdoors writers. Each year he spends more than 150 days in the field. He has written for such national publications as *Outside* magazine and is a regular columnist for Maine's *Northwoods Sporting Journal*.

For the last ten years Hanrahan has spent nearly one-third of the year outside. A lifelong hunter and fisherman, Hanrahan's outdoor life began at Boy Scout camps in upstate New York and Vermont. In fall, the author lives in remote outpost camps in the North Maine Woods, a three-million-acre tract that is the eastern United States' largest wilderness parcel.

A master Maine guide, Hanrahan is a graduate of Princeton University. Before coming to Maine, he worked as a reporter and columnist for the *New York Daily News*. His work has been honored by the New York Press Association and the Maine Press Association, as well as the Maine Association of Broadcasters.

A resident of Whitefield, Hanrahan has also worked as a small farmer and dairy farm helper.

The author is a sporting clays enthusiast. He is married to Lisa Levinson, a frequent outdoors companion and accomplished camp cook.

KELLY THORNDIKE was born and raised in Midcoast Maine. A self-educated artist and illustrator, he is a student of Winslow Homer, N. C. Wyeth, Frank Benson, and Louise Nevelson.

He is a combat-wounded Iraq war veteran and a recipient of the Purple Heart. This is his first professional project since returning from Iraq in 2004, where he suffered brain injury. He credits the kindness and patience of close friends and family and the very professional, often youthful, team of caregivers at Togus VA Medical Center in Augusta, Maine, for making it possible for him to be creative again.

The artist and illustrator met author Tom Hanrahan at Spencer Pond Camps, a sporting camp in the Big Woods. Both share a love of the outdoors.

On Cross Island, off Machias